intelligence quest

Project-Based Learning and Multiple Intelligences

WALTER McKENZIE

International Society for Technology in Education

EUGENE, OREGON • WASHINGTON, DC

intelligence quest

Project-Based Learning and Multiple Intelligences

WALTER McKENZIE

© 2012 International Society for Technology in Education
World rights reserved. No part of this book may be reproduced or transmitted in any form or by any means—electronic, mechanical, photocopying, recording, or by any information storage or retrieval system—without prior written permission from the publisher. Contact Permissions Editor: www.iste.org/learn/publications/permissions-and-reprints.aspx; permissions@iste.org; fax: 1.541.302.3780.

Director of Book Publishing: *Courtney Burkholder*
Acquisitions Editor: *Jeff V. Bolkan*
Production Editors: *Lynda Gansel, Tina Wells*
Production Coordinator: *Rachel Williams*
Graphic Designer: *Signe Landin*
Copy Editor and Proofreader: *Katherine Gries*
Cover Design, Book Design, and Production: *Kim McGovern*

Library of Congress Cataloging-in-Publication Data

McKenzie, Walter.
    Intelligence quest : project-based learning and multiple intelligences / Walter McKenzie. — 1st ed.
      p. cm.
    ISBN 978-1-56484-309-8 (pbk.)
    1. Project method in teaching. 2. Multiple intelligences.   I. Title.
    LB1027.43.M35 2012
    371.3'6—dc23

                                         2011051286

Curr

First Edition
ISBN: 978-1-56484-309-8
Printed in the United States of America

Cover and Inside Art: © istockphoto.com/Stefanie Timmermann
ISTE® is a registered trademark of the International Society for Technology in Education.

SUSTAINABLE FORESTRY INITIATIVE — Certified Sourcing — www.sfiprogram.org — SFI-00341 — Label applies to the text stock

About ISTE

The International Society for Technology in Education (ISTE) is the trusted source for professional development, knowledge generation, advocacy, and leadership for innovation. ISTE is the premier membership association for educators and education leaders engaged in improving teaching and learning by advancing the effective use of technology in PK–12 and teacher education.

Home to ISTE's annual conference and exposition, the ISTE leadership conference, and the widely adopted NETS, ISTE represents more than 100,000 professionals worldwide. We support our members with information, networking opportunities, and guidance as they face the challenge of transforming education. To find out more about these and other ISTE initiatives, visit our website at www.iste.org.

As part of our mission, ISTE Book Publishing works with experienced educators to develop and produce practical resources for classroom teachers, teacher educators, and technology leaders. Every manuscript we select for publication is carefully peer-reviewed and professionally edited. We value your feedback on this book and other ISTE products. Email us at books@iste.org.

International Society for Technology in Education
Washington, DC, Office:
    1710 Rhode Island Ave. NW, Suite 900, Washington, DC 20036-3132
Eugene, Oregon, Office:
    180 West 8th Ave., Suite 300, Eugene, OR 97401-2916
Order Desk: 1.800.336.5191
Order Fax: 1.541.302.3778
Customer Service: orders@iste.org
Book Publishing: books@iste.org
Book Sales and Marketing: booksmarketing@iste.org
Web: www.iste.org

About the Author

Walter McKenzie is a lifelong learner, teacher, leader, and connector. Currently the Director of Constituent Services for ASCD, Walter served 25 years in public schools: 14 years as a classroom teacher and 11 years as a district coordinator, director, and assistant superintendent. He also served as a senior technology training specialist for the Department of Housing and Urban Development in Washington, D.C., and in its field offices around the nation.

Walter is an internationally known presenter on multiple intelligences theory and instructional technology, and he has published various books and articles regarding these subjects. He has been instrumental in launching and leading online professional development programs and postgraduate professional education courses around the country. He has actively facilitated online educator communities and web-based interdisciplinary instructional projects through his One and Only Surfaquarium (http://surfaquarium.com) over the past 15 years.

Contents

preface

E ducation in the digital age demands a new paradigm. In today's world doctors, scientists, and engineers are evolving in their practices through the application and benefits of new technologies. Teachers must also make this shift. Students need access to all kinds of technologies and a variety of experiences for making use of them. Not rote, artificial experiences; not didactic, how-to experiences; but meaningful, authentic, real-world experiences that match the demands of the 21st-century workplace.

Our challenge as educators is to provide an education that is consistent with our students' digital-age experience. To accomplish this you don't have to be up on every new trend, application, and gadget. Rather, teachers must holistically reconsider the way they design and manage their learning environments—their classrooms—so that they are conducive to the ubiquitous technology of our time.

My work with Howard Gardner's theory of multiple intelligences has provided the opportunity to integrate technological advances with Gardner's nine intelligences—or "ways of learning"—in ways that will expand and improve teaching techniques. In this book I present an instructional model called the Intelligence Quest (IQuest), which offers a flexible approach to supporting the new digital education paradigm. The IQuest addresses all nine intelligences identified in Gardner's pioneering work, while providing a clear structure and specific goals for your Information Age classroom. Whether you are known among your colleagues as an early adopter of new instructional techniques or you are more cautious in your approach, the IQuest can help you to restructure your thinking in all facets of instruction—from simple read-and-respond activities to full-fledged technology-infused projects.

It is my hope that the IQuest model will push your thinking, prompt you into further discussion, and empower you to help your students make connections to real-world working definitions of productivity.

CHAPTER 1

IQuest
A New Paradigm for a New Age

Today's world demands a new educational paradigm. Educators are inundated by new technologies that promise to improve education in myriad ways, we know more than ever about how human intelligence works, and there is a greater need than ever for authentic learning experiences that engage students. We need to design a classroom culture and contexts that support a variety of learning styles while incorporating the effective use of ever-evolving technologies.

This new paradigm would include the following tenets:

- All students are unique learners
- One approach to instruction does not meet the needs of all learners

- Learner motivation is fueled by intrinsic interests, values, and attitudes
- Skills and concepts should be presented in multiple modes and contexts
- Today's classroom is preparing students for the 21st-century workplace
- Classroom management requires greater learner autonomy
- Students should be immersed in authentic tasks and assessments
- Creativity and diversity are celebrated
- There is more than one way to solve a problem
- Collaborative problem-solving in a student-centered classroom is the goal
- Technology tools help teachers and students achieve this goal

The Intelligence Quest, or IQuest, based on Howard Gardner's (1999) Multiple Intelligences (MI) theory, offers a flexible framework to support this new paradigm. The IQuest framework can help you to restructure your thinking in all facets of instruction, from simple read-and-respond activities to full-fledged technology-infused projects. Lessons in an IQuest format address all the intelligences identified in the pioneering work of Gardner while providing a clear structure and specific goals for your Information Age classroom.

Gardner's MI theory can help teachers make use of new technologies in ways that transcend their own MI comfort zones and expand their instructional repertoire, transforming their classrooms into authentic, connected, real-world learning zones.

It is no coincidence that multiple intelligences theory and digital technology have evolved concurrently over the last 50 years.

They very much go hand-in-hand. It is the development of new technologies that has helped us to better understand the inner workings of the human brain. And it is the growing body of work on artificial intelligence that has helped us to understand human intelligence in more intricate, sophisticated ways. In the same way, multiple intelligences theory and technology are complementary tools for instruction. A working understanding of the intelligences provides for appropriate, effective media selection in the classroom. And the explosion of educational technologies makes it much more possible to accommodate all the different paths to learning in the classroom.

How can teachers start moving to this new paradigm? First, recognize the ways you were taught as a student. Embrace them and appreciate them for the time in which they served you well. Then let them go and move on.

Think of the greatest teachers you ever had. Do you think they would still be using chalk on slate if they had access to the kinds of tools we have at our disposal today? Great teachers adapt and learn throughout their lives. Great teachers are never satisfied with yesterday's success. Rather than holding fast to an old paradigm, they help explore and define the new shift in thinking.

Honor those innovative teachers who instilled in you a love for learning and a desire to be a teacher yourself; carry on their legacy as a pioneer and innovator in your own time.

Leaving the Comfort Zone

The role of teachers is changing. Twenty years ago constructivism pushed us to move away from being the disseminators of knowledge to being the facilitators of learning. In today's world that is no longer enough. Beyond facilitation, teachers today need to be modelers of learning—understanding, synthesizing, creating, and problem solving right in there with their students; everyone inquiring and discovering and building meaning together.

Educators naturally tend to teach and develop instruction in ways that focus on their own intelligence strengths; this becomes their MI comfort zone. But in a thoughtful invitation to educators everywhere, Leila Christenbury (2010) asks "When is it time for teachers to leave their comfort zone?" This reminded me of a favorite truism: "There's no learning in the comfort zone, and no comfort in the learning zone." It has been used for years to inspire teachers to think about the affective component to learning. Merging these two ideas together means we need to have our thinking challenged in order to learn new ideas. I believe the best teachers are lifelong learners. Lifelong learners push themselves outside of their comfort zones on a regular basis as they continue to learn, grow and adapt. This is especially important in this age of fast-paced change.

There is a connection between how we learn and how we teach. Our learning style impacts our teaching style. Being a lifelong learner is actually a style of teaching. But can you learn and teach at the same time? Do you have a learning-teaching style? What if your learning-teaching style is a toggle switch, and while you are in the one mode you cannot be in the other? Think about it … if you are learning something new, don't you have to reach a certain point of mastery before you can switch gears into a teaching mode? Or even more to the point: in learning, we are open and receptive to information and stimuli and experience; in teaching is the converse true? And if it's not, in an age of quickly-changing information and technology, shouldn't teaching mode also require us to be open and receptive to information and stimuli and experience, even as we are teaching?

I propose we modify the truism I stated above to: "There's no teaching in the comfort zone, and no comfort in the teaching zone." If you infer from this statement what I do, your mind might now be processing questions such as:

- If I learn out of my comfort zone, does that mean it should be easier for me to teach out of my comfort zone? Feels like that doesn't necessarily follow...

- As an excellent teacher in this day and age, should I constantly be pushing myself out of my teaching comfort zone in order to model 21st-century skills for my students?

- Should I not be too comfortable with the strategies, methodologies, and resources with which I have been successful in the classroom?

- Does that mean the most appropriate way to meet the needs of each student is to leave my comfort zone to meet them in each of theirs? Or do both teacher and learner need to be uncomfortable? Whose comfort zone is it anyway?

The structure of the IQuest lends itself to pushing you out of your comfort zone (relying on your natural intelligence strengths) and helping you develop instruction that will stimulate all the intelligences in operation in your classroom. Through each combination of intelligences in the examples in this book, you will explore and consider how you can extend your instructional expertise in ways that accommodate all the intelligences.

Meaningful Use of Technology

Teachers are facing an influx of new technologies. The tendency is to get excited about these technologies and then look for ways to implement them into existing instruction. This is important—we need innovators to explore the possibilities of technology. But there is also the need for models of how to be successful in using technology in instruction, models that are sustainable and replicable in classrooms everywhere. To be effective, these models need to first focus on learning for understanding, not on the technology tools themselves.

There is a need to use technology in focused meaningful ways, as opposed to using it just because we can. Mastery of content, skills, and processes stays with students for a lifetime; the "coolness factor" of the technologies they use fades away.

The IQuest framework can be used to design lessons that connect technology to lessons seamlessly and incidentally. When designed well, technology-infused instruction is a naturally occurring series of learning opportunities in the classroom. A good friend is fond of saying, "the map in your hand should match the view on the ground." Instruction should be that map, and your classroom should be learning's ground zero.

If we first identify the ways we want to reach students and the ways in which we want them to demonstrate understanding, then the appropriate technologies will make themselves evident. When you consider using a technology in the classroom, here's a good test: Ask yourself, "Is this technology being selected for my teaching preference or my students' learning success?" If it is your teaching technology of choice, you may want to step back and reassess your instructional priorities.

Focus on Affective Aspect of Learning

In an age that espouses the notion that all children can learn, the tests and teaching strategies we use in education continue to neglect the affective aspect of learning. From the dawn of standardized testing, the focus has always been on mastering content because content mastery is easy to measure. The Bloom Commission (Bloom et al., 1956) identified affective and psychomotor educational objectives, but it is the cognitive objectives that have received attention over the past 40 years.

An IQuest allows learners to truly take ownership of their learning and identify how and why what they learn is important, leading students to achieve at levels far beyond rote memorization of content. If they can internalize what they see and imagine what is not readily evident, and if they can make connections from what they experience personally to larger truths, then all learners can be successful not only in school but throughout their lives.

But how do you get your hands around the personal aspect of learning? Gardner's model of human cognition does just that.

Multiple Intelligences

Before discussing the IQuest further, I would like to make several points about MI theory in education, the foundation upon which the IQuest rests. Howard Gardner's work has long been extremely popular among educators and is often viewed as the antithesis of current trends in testing and accountability. In reality, MI is not the antithesis of accountability. It is not simply a feel-good theory, an "I'm OK—you're OK" rationalization of what we have always done as teachers. If we view it that way, we completely short-sell its potential to transform teaching and learning in the Information Age.

Rather, MI provides for us a framework for understanding all the paths to learning so that all learners can be successful. And the explosion of educational technologies makes it much more possible to accommodate all the different paths to learning in the classroom. The best teachers have been accommodating all the intelligences with their learners for years, even before Gardner gave them a name, and including those intelligences not usually valued in traditional academic tracks. This continues to be true of so many teachers working outside of the mainstream, from vocational and trade classrooms to special education and alternative education settings. This accommodation of all the intelligences can often be seen in the primary grades, where teachers frequently provide learning experiences that are multisensory and multimedial in nature. There are pockets of MI in action in every school open today. With all we know about the human mind, we have an obligation to nurture those pockets of activity and encourage them to overflow across our schools. The IQuest is a highly effective way to ensure this nurturing and encouragement occurs for all learners, in all subjects, at all levels.

Let's examine Gardner's nine intelligences, either as a brushup or an introduction:

Spatial: seeing, imagining, and organizing ideas spatially. This intelligence is stimulated by seeing concepts in action in order to understand them, as well as the ability to "see" things in one's mind. Also referred to as Visual/Spatial.

Linguistic: communicating ideas through the spoken and written word. This includes speaking, reading, and writing and has been traditionally valued through classroom lecture and discussion, as well as textbooks and worksheets. Also referred to as Verbal/Linguistic.

Logical: reasoning and problem solving. This is key in making sense of complex sets of data and employing strategies that make use of that data to complete meaningful tasks. Also referred to as Mathematical/Logical.

Kinesthetic: interaction with one's environment. This intelligence promotes understanding through concrete experience, which can include fine and gross motor tasks that promote understanding of skills and concepts. Also referred to as Bodily/Kinesthetic.

Rhythmic: patterns, rhythms, and sound. This includes not only auditory learning, but the identification of patterns in data through all the senses. Also referred to as Musical/ Rhythmical.

Intrapersonal: feelings, values, and attitudes. This is a decidedly affective component of learning through which students place value on what they learn and take ownership for their learning.

Interpersonal: interaction with others. This intelligence promotes the social aspect of understanding through interaction, collaboration, and feedback while working cooperatively with others.

Naturalist: classification, categories, and hierarchies. This intelligence picks up on subtle differences in meaning, making distinctions that can be used to organize information into schematic frameworks.

Existential: making connections to the "big picture": This intelligence seeks contexts for real world understandings and applications of new learning. This includes personal, communal, and curricular connections.

Understanding the basic definition of each intelligence is important, but not as important as the working understanding of how the intelligences work with one another. After all, if these different paths to learning always act in concert, we're really not providing for the full potential of this model unless we look at all of the intelligences in operation together.

This can be difficult to do, because once you begin observing a specific student the intelligences become very fluid and free flowing. What might be easily recognizable in isolation becomes much less clear when observing the intelligences in action holistically.

When Gardner's theory is presented to educators, teachers always come up with questions about this overlapping of intelligences. We are so used to theory that nicely packages teaching and learning into neat compartments, we tend to cling to the individual integrity of each intelligence. It's hard to let go and accept the fact that since Gardner's theory is based on the way these intelligences actually function within human cognition, it's a little less easy to compartmentalize and parcel out in tight, tidy packages. However, once teachers get past the traditional definition of intelligence, there are powerful new possibilities for learning in the classroom.

When you look at the nine intelligences, what common traits do you see? What are the similarities among their unique traits? How can we make sense of nine different paths to learning? This is the real challenge teachers face as they implement Gardner's model in instruction.

Multiple Intelligence Domains

In my 2005 book, *Multiple Intelligences and Instructional Technology*, I modified Gardner's list of intelligences by breaking it into three intelligence domains:

- Analytic domain
- Introspective domain
- Interactive domain

Each of these domains comprises three of Gardner's intelligences. This structure will allow you to more easily accommodate all nine intelligences in the classroom. (See Figure 1.1.) By organizing and planning for these intelligence domains in specific sequences, learning experiences—IQuests—can be crafted that provide all the necessary conditions for successful learning.

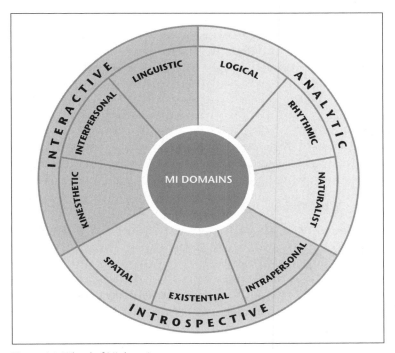

Figure 1.1. Wheel of MI domains

These domains that I have created serve as organizers for understanding the fluid relationship of all nine intelligences. They are meant to align the intelligences with familiar learner attributes teachers routinely observe in the classroom.

Getting Started with IQuests

The IQuest framework incorporates the value of today's ubiquitous technologies with best instructional practices for the classroom. Students are challenged to think, ask questions, problem solve, and create new understandings as they are engaged in meaningful, authentic learning tasks. While this book is replete with ideas and examples, the true value of the IQuest is that you can easily adapt it to meet your own needs as a teacher. It is a framework for effectively, appropriately incorporating technology into instruction seamlessly and incidentally so that the focus is on learning productively rather than how to operate hardware and applications.

Working understanding of the intelligences provides for appropriate, effective media selection in the classroom. Chapters 2, 3, and 4 contain detailed information about each of the intelligence domains, and also answer the following questions:

- What are the core characteristics of this intelligence?
- How does this intelligence exhibit itself in learners?
- How do teachers and technologies support this intelligence?

Chapter 5 takes an in-depth look at the IQuest framework and how it can be adapted for use with virtually any subject matter, in any classroom. It also provides step-by-step instructions on the process and implementation of your own IQuests. Chapters 6–11 provide descriptions of six types of IQuests (highlighting the structure and characteristics of each by showing a working example) and list correlation to the ISTE NETS for Students.

References

Bloom, B. S. (Ed.), Engelhart, M. D., Furst, E. J., Hill, W. H., & Krathwohl, D. R. (1956). *Taxonomy of educational objectives: Handbook I: Cognitive domain.* New York, NY: David McKay.

Christenbury, L. (2010, December 1). Time to leave the comfort zone: Adjusting teaching to student needs [Blog post]. Retrieved from http://ascd. typepad.com/blog/2010/12/time-to-leave-the-comfort-zone.html

Gardner, H. (1999). *Intelligence reframed: Multiple intelligences for the 21st century.* New York, NY: Basic Books.

McKenzie, W. (2005). *Multiple intelligences and instructional technology* (2nd ed.). Eugene, OR: International Society for Technology in Education.

CHAPTER 2

thinking critically
The Analytic Domain of Intelligences

The traditional focus of education has been critical thinking: the ability to reason, make sense of information, and solve problems. If we were to identify those intelligences that serve this purpose, which would they be? Which of Gardner's nine intelligences best fit into a domain of critical thinking? Obviously, the logical intelligence is a strong candidate with its emphasis on reasoning and problem solving. What other intelligences augment these logic-driven processes?

Consider the rhythmic intelligence as a second intelligence that promotes critical thinking. Once patterns have been identified, how does the mind organize information into manageable frameworks? The naturalist intelligence is a pathway to organized understanding and recall of data.

In each of these three intelligences—the logical, rhythmic, and naturalist—understanding takes place through an analysis of information as it is encountered, whether naturally or by design. Even though they can have connections to and overlap with the other intelligences, these three most fundamentally promote the process of analyzing and incorporating data into existing schema, and are by their nature heuristic processes. For these reasons, they are grouped into the analytic domain of intelligence.

How might teachers and technologies support the intelligences in the analytic domain? Let's take a closer look.

Logical Intelligence

The logical intelligence supports critical thinking through its linear, sequential approach to making sense of information and orderly, methodical approach to accomplishing tasks.

Core Characteristics:

- Linear Reasoning—seeking order and consistency in the world

- Concrete Reasoning—breaking down systems into their components

- Abstract Reasoning—using symbols that represent concrete ideas

- Causal Relationships—identifying cause and effect within a system

- Complex Operations—performing sophisticated algorithms

Students with a strong logical intelligence:

- Seek order
- Reason scientifically
- Identify relationships
- Enjoy testing theories
- Like completing puzzles
- Excel at calculating numbers
- Solve problems instinctively
- Analyze abstract ideas
- Manipulate functions
- Perform these operations at a rapid rate

Teachers support this intelligence in the classroom by:

- Creating intrinsic and extrinsic order in the classroom
- Presenting criteria at the beginning of an activity to provide structure
- Offering open-ended problem-solving tasks
- Including convergent thinking activities in instruction
- Promoting experiments that test student hypotheses
- Using syllogisms in language
- Encouraging classroom debate
- Incorporating puzzles into learning centers
- Setting short term, achievable goals for the class
- Allowing students to participate in building assessment rubrics

Instructional technologies that stimulate this intelligence include:

- Lectures
- Cuisenaire rods

- Unifix cubes
- Tangrams
- Measuring cups
- Measuring scales
- Rulers/yardsticks
- Slide rules
- Graphing calculators
- Spreadsheets
- Search engines
- Directories
- FTP clients
- Gophers
- WebQuests
- Problem-solving tasks
- Programming languages

Rhythmic Intelligence

The rhythmic intelligence supports critical thinking through its ability to encounter random stimuli and make sense of it by detecting regular, identifiable sequences of data.

Core Characteristics:

- Aural Orientation—heightened listening ability
- Patterning—seeking all kinds of patterns through the five senses
- Resonance—identification with patterns as an expression of experience
- Audiation—internalizing and recalling information through sound

Students with a strong rhythmic intelligence:

- Seek patterns in new information
- Find patterns in their environment
- Are particularly drawn to sound
- Respond to cadence in language
- Enjoy moving to rhythms
- Pick up terms and phrases in foreign languages easily
- Use patterning to both internalize and recall skills, ideas, and concepts

Teachers support this intelligence in the classroom by providing:

- Manipulatives
- Rich sounds in the environment
- Opportunities to move to rhythm
- Visual patterns
- Immersion in a foreign language
- Varied rhyme schemes
- Patterns in sequences of numbers
- Symphony recordings
- Codes to decipher
- Sheet music to read

Instructional technologies that stimulate this intelligence include:

- Pattern blocks
- Puzzles
- Musical instruments
- Phonograph
- Headphones/ear buds

- Audio player/recorder
- Digital sounds
- Online pattern games
- Multimedia presentations
- Online video sites (such as YouTube)
- Speakers
- CD/DVD discs and players
- Podcasting

Naturalist Intelligence

The naturalist intelligence supports critical thinking through its ability to create mental constructs that make sense of patterns of information. Through processes of classifying, categorizing, and prioritizing information into meaningful hierarchies in the mind, the naturalist intelligence helps to make critical thinking possible.

Core Characteristics:

- Natural Orientation—identification with living organisms and their environments
- Attribute Orientation—finding common traits among items
- Categorization—identifying categories by attribute
- Hierarchical Reasoning—ranking items by significance and relationship
- Schematic Memory—internalizing and recalling information by attribute, category, or hierarchy

Students with a strong naturalist intelligence:

- Are intrinsically organized
- Demonstrate an empathy with nature
- Pick up on subtle differences in meaning
- Like to make collections of materials
- Enjoy sorting and organizing materials
- Impose their own sense of order on new information
- Respond to semantic mapping activities
- Enjoy using charts, tables, diagrams, and timelines

Teachers support this intelligence in the classroom by:

- Using graphic organizers
- Providing sorting and attribute-grouping tasks
- Brainstorming categories
- Charting hierarchies
- Utilizing semantic mapping of ideas
- Building portfolios of student work
- Making connections to the natural world
- Modeling strategies for finding common attributes, categories and hierarchies across the curriculum

Instructional technologies that stimulate this intelligence include:

- Magnifying glass
- Microscope
- Telescope
- Bug box
- Scrapbook
- Sandwich bag

- Plastic container
- Database
- DVD
- USB portable storage device
- File manager
- Semantic mapping tools

Application of the Analytic Domain

Let's consider Ms. Ortiz's class. They have created instruments that simulate the sounds of the rain forest, and each student is now creating his or her own composition that makes use of these sounds. As each student comes before the class to present and conduct his or her composition, the other students must follow the patterns of sound and imitate them accurately in order to successfully perform the piece. There is a careful auditory analysis of each rhythm presented to the class, and in cases where the student has created sheet music with symbols for each of the different instruments as they play, there is visual analysis of patterns evident as well.

Then there's Min and Hakim, who are working to create a bridge out of popsicle sticks that will be able to hold the weight of a motorized 12-pound truck as it crosses their structure. They have studied many kinds of bridges and they are employing what they have learned to make a structure strong enough to successfully do the job. As they attempt different designs, they are careful to analyze their failures and build on their successes. After two weeks of working a little every day, Min and Hakim come up with a design that is effective in safely holding the truck's weight.

Finally, consider Melissa, who is sorting leaves by different attributes at a first grade learning center. She sorts them by color, then by size, then by texture. As she comes up with a classification system for the leaves that makes sense to her, she glues each leaf down on a large sheet of paper that serves as an organizer. She then presents her leaf classification system to be displayed in the classroom so that students can compare and contrast one another's strategies for classification.

The analytic domain is in play in all of these examples. Are there other intelligences also evident in these examples? Of course! All of the intelligences are in operation all of the time. But by harnessing the power of the analytic intelligences in one domain, teachers can focus on their potential for helping all students to succeed. Having a working knowledge of this domain is essential in utilizing the IQuest effectively.

reflection

1. How are the analytic intelligences supported in your instructional repertoire?

2. How can new technologies accommodate the logical intelligence beyond mathematics?

3. What potential does mobile computing hold for the naturalist intelligence?

4. How can portable digital audio stimulate the rhythmic intelligence across the curriculum?

CHAPTER 3

thinking within
The Introspective Domain of Intelligences

W hich of the intelligences best fit into a domain of personal understanding? The spatial intelligence is a strong candidate, with its emphasis on visualizing, imagining, and spatially organizing ideas and concepts. Once one can internalize the world using spatial intelligence, it is a natural extension to imagine beyond what is seen. This is the source of hopes and dreams, the impetus behind all achievement. What other intelligences support the personal component of human cognition?

Consider the intrapersonal intelligence as a distinct path to learning that taps into personal understanding. Intrapersonal intelligence helps students to make an affective connection with the curriculum. To learn to solve quadratic equations is a valuable skill in isolation, but to know when and how to use it in everyday life makes it meaningful and useful beyond discrete mathematics.

What about the connection between personal learning and the larger world around us? Consider the existential intelligence as the final facet of the introspective domain. By making connections across subjects and experience, learning has a greater depth of understanding. From family and community to world and universe, the existential intelligence helps us connect to the larger truths of life.

In each of these three intelligences—the spatial, intrapersonal, and existential—understanding takes place by attaching meaning and value to the content that must be mastered. While there is overlap with all the intelligences, these three specifically attach affective connection to learning so that achievement is optimal. For these reasons, they are grouped into the introspective domain of intelligence.

How might teachers and technologies support the intelligences in the introspective domain? Let's take a closer look.

Spatial Intelligence

The spatial intelligence supports personal thinking by allowing learners to internalize and manipulate the world around them.

Core Characteristics:

- Spatial Awareness—solving problems using spatial orientation
- Non-Sequential Reasoning—thinking in divergent ways
- Visual Acuity—assessment of information based on principles of design and aesthetics

- Imagination—seeing the possibilities before engaging them in the physical world
- Small motor coordination—creating, building, arranging, decorating

Students with a strong spatial intelligence:

- Seek ocular stimulation
- Respond to color, line, and shape
- Can "see" ideas in their minds
- Use mental images for mnemonic devices
- Imagine possibilities
- Enjoy expressing themselves through the arts
- Appreciate symmetry and congruence
- Enjoy rearranging their environment
- Can manipulate 3-D models in their minds
- Understand by seeing a concept in action

Teachers support this intelligence in the classroom by:

- Allowing student movement around the learning environment
- Providing a visually stimulating environment
- Sketching plans before beginning work
- Brainstorming ideas
- Using semantic mapping
- Conducting guided imagery exercises
- Working with manipulatives
- Diagramming abstract concepts
- Providing visual assessment performance tasks
- Using visual technologies such as Kid Pix and PowerPoint

Instructional technologies that stimulate this intelligence include:

- Projector
- Television
- Video
- Picture books
- Art supplies
- Chalkboard
- Dry erase board
- Slide shows
- Charting and graphing
- Monitor
- Digital camera/camcorder
- Scanner
- Graphics editor
- HTML editor
- Digital animation
- Digital movies

Intrapersonal Intelligence

The intrapersonal intelligence allows learners to connect learning to their own personal interests, values, and attitudes.

Core Characteristics:

- Affective Awareness—the knowledge of one's feelings, attitudes, and outlook
- Ethical Awareness—the setting of one's principles and moral priorities

- Self-Regulation—monitoring one's thoughts, actions, and behavior
- Metacognition—the awareness of one's thought processes

Students with a strong intrapersonal intelligence:
- Are comfortable with themselves
- Express strong like or dislike of particular activities
- Communicate their feelings
- Sense their own strengths and weaknesses
- Show confidence in their abilities
- Set realistic goals
- Make appropriate choices
- Follow their instincts
- Express a sense of justice and fairness
- Relate to others based on their sense of self

Teachers support this intelligence in the classroom by:
- Differentiating instruction
- Using analogies in making comparisons
- Providing activities that offer learner choices
- Having students set goals for themselves in the classroom
- Including daily journal writing in the classroom routine
- Providing opportunities for learners to express their feelings on a topic
- Allowing opportunities for student reflection on learning
- Examining current events in terms of social justice

- Including student self-assessment in classroom assessment strategies
- Utilizing interest inventories, questionnaires, interviews, and other approaches to measuring student growth

Instructional technologies that stimulate this intelligence include:

- Journals
- Diaries
- Surveys
- Voting machines
- Learning centers
- Children's literature
- Class discussion
- Real-time projects
- Online surveys
- Online forms
- Digital portfolios
- Self-assessments

Existential Intelligence

The existential intelligence supports personal learning by making connections from spatial and intrapersonal knowing to understanding of the global context of our existence.

Core Characteristics:

- Collective Consciousness—the capability to see how something relates to the big picture
- Collective Values—the understanding of classical values of truth, goodness, and beauty

- Summative Iteration—the ability to summarize details into a larger understanding
- Intuitive Iteration—a responsiveness to the intangible qualities of being human, be it responding to the arts, philosophical virtues, or religious tenets

Students with a strong existential intelligence:

- Seek meaningful learning
- Look for connections across the curriculum
- Like to synthesize ideas based on their learning
- Enjoy literature and customs from other cultures
- Have a strong connection with family and friends
- Develop a strong identity with their neighborhoods and towns
- Express a sense of belonging to a global community
- Like to get involved with social and political causes
- Can have a strong commitment to their health and well-being
- Tend to look at information relative to the context in which it is presented

Teachers support this intelligence in the classroom by:

- Offering an overview before starting new instruction
- Considering topics from multiple points of view
- Relating material to global themes and concepts
- Integrating instruction across the curriculum
- Including the arts in instruction where appropriate
- Discussing how topics are important to the classroom, school, community, or world

- Bringing in resource people who offer additional perspective on a topic
- Helping students learn to cohesively summarize what they have learned
- Allowing students to demonstrate learning by applying understanding in new and different contexts
- Having students participate in rubric development for performance-based tasks so that they take ownership for their learning

Instructional technologies that stimulate this intelligence include:

- Art replica
- Planetarium
- Stage drama
- Classic literature
- Classic philosophy
- Symbols of world religions
- Virtual communities
- Virtual art exhibits
- Virtual field trips
- Social media sites
- Blogs
- Wikis
- Virtual reality
- Simulations

Application of the Introspective Domain

Consider Michelangelo celebrating the discovery of a large slab of marble because he wants to free the angel encased therein through his act of sculpting. There is a uniquely emotional component to envisioning a piece of art before the artist actually creates it. In the same way, recall a student you have worked with who served as a class leader simply because she was able to visualize where she wanted to go with a project before the rest of the group even got its collective self together to begin discussing the possibilities. There is an intuitive release of energy that sparks the enthusiasm and imagination of others when the spatial intelligence is unleashed.

The existential intelligence displays similar affective characteristics. When Søren Kierkegaard described looking at the infinite depth of the night sky and having an emotionally charged response—"Yes, I am part of something bigger in the universe!"—he was referring to this experience. It is necessary to make that leap of faith in order to contribute to the collective human experience. By the same token, place yourself in the presence of the Pieta and feel the emotional response as your senses take in the aesthetic beauty of one of mankind's great expressions of human love and suffering. It moves many unsuspecting onlookers to tears. This is another example of that emotional response to cognitive stimulus.

The intrapersonal intelligence may be the most obvious example of this. Consider 14-year-old Jacqueline, who filters everything she is learning through her strong sense of social justice. She lights up when learning about the plight of Native Americans in the 19th century, the ethical dilemmas presented by genetic engineering, and reading Alan Paton's *Cry, the Beloved Country*. In fact, with an upcoming presidential election in the fall, Jacqueline is very interested in helping out at her local party headquarters and campaigning for the candidates of her choice. Everything Jacqueline is learning is reinforced and mastered by the emotional connection she has with the different kinds of content she is studying.

These three intelligences are introspective because they require a looking inward by the learner, an emotive connection to their own experiences and beliefs in order to make sense of new learning. Again, all the intelligences are in play in any authentic task. To know which intelligences are being emphasized in a learning task, look to the learning objective. The objective will point to the intelligences that are the focus of a lesson. By compartmentalizing the introspective intelligences into one domain, teachers can concentrate on the affective component of learning to help all students to succeed. Tapping into the introspective domain is critical in utilizing the IQuest effectively.

reflection

1. How are the introspective intelligences supported in your instructional repertoire?

2. How will digital video transform the Information Age classroom?

3. Which new technologies hold the most promise for accommodating the existential intelligence in the classroom?

4. In what ways will the intrapersonal intelligence help define education in the Information Age?

CHAPTER 4

thinking outward
The Interactive Domain of Intelligences

W hen all is said and done, learning and demonstrating understanding is best showcased in hands-on situations. Taking risks, testing assumptions, and interacting with our surroundings are the stuff of real-world productivity. When Gardner defines intelligence as "the ability to solve problems and create products of value in one's own culture" this is what he has in mind. Sure, the analytic and introspective intelligences are key in the holistic process of learning, but from early on we are doers by nature—the proof is in the doing.

This has been an issue in the traditional classroom. If a learner's intelligence strengths were not verbal and logical, that student would be handicapped in both learning and assessment performance. Put that same learner in an environment where all the intelligences are exercised and valued, and it's a level playing field where everyone can be successful. Being empowered to interact with language, with others, and with the learning environment is incredibly liberating. Suddenly the possibilities are endless, in the classroom and beyond.

The remaining three intelligences nicely fill out this third domain of active learning. The linguistic intelligence, though traditionally valued in education, is nonetheless a powerful conduit for active learning through speaking, reading, and writing. Using the many forms of language to negotiate and express understanding is critical in building mastery-level knowledge.

Consider the kinesthetic intelligence as another realm that promotes interactive learning. Hands-on learning in its many forms is the most common form of performance task, and the easiest to assess by peer and teacher observation. Unfortunately, as students move higher in their academic careers, the less opportunity they are given to exercise their kinesthetic intelligence. If we are committed to accommodating all the intelligences in our classrooms, this must change.

Finally, the interpersonal intelligence rounds out the domain of active learning with its emphasis on interaction with others. Through peer conferencing, pair-sharing, cooperative groups, and collaborative projects, learning takes on a social dimension that takes learning to a higher level of understanding. Practice of successful interactions will strengthen every student's learning experience.

The three interactive intelligences—linguistic, kinesthetic, and interpersonal—make learning action-oriented. While all three domains are crucial in ensuring success for all learners, these three intelligences make learning a practical, real-world experience. For these reasons, they are grouped as the interactive domain of intelligence.

How might teachers and technologies support the intelligences in the interactive domain? Let's take a closer look.

Linguistic Intelligence

The linguistic intelligence supports active learning by allowing students to implement the many different functions of language.

Core Characteristics:

- Ideation—ability to think and remember through internal language
- Functional Literacy—ability to understand the rules and functions of language
- Self-Regulation—can analyze one's own use of language
- Adaptation—can apply rules of language to new and different contexts
- Oral Expression—ability to explain and express thoughts verbally
- Written Expression—ability to explain and express thoughts in writing

Students with a strong linguistic intelligence:

- Appreciate the subtleties of grammar and definitions
- Spell easily
- Enjoy word games
- Understand jokes, puns, and riddles
- Use descriptive language

- Are good storytellers
- Internalize new information through lecture and discussion
- Demonstrate understanding easily through discussion and essay

Teachers support this intelligence in the classroom by:

- Exploring new vocabulary
- Teaching terms and expressions from other languages
- Encouraging opportunities for public speaking
- Incorporating drama into learning
- Making daily journals a part of the curriculum
- Promoting opportunities for creative writing
- Nurturing oral storytelling
- Including opportunities for expository and narrative writing
- Using quality children's and young adult literature in the classroom

Instructional technologies that stimulate this intelligence include:

- Textbook
- Pen/pencil
- Worksheet
- Newspaper
- Magazine
- Word processing
- Electronic mail
- Desktop publishing
- Web-based publishing

- Keyboard
- Speech recognition devices
- Text bridges

Kinesthetic Intelligence

The kinesthetic intelligence is the one stimulated by active, physical interaction with one's environment.

Core Characteristics:

- Sensory—internalizes information through bodily sensation
- Reflexive—responds quickly and intuitively to physical stimulus
- Tactile—demonstrates well-developed gross and/or fine motor skills
- Concrete—expresses feelings and ideas through body movement
- Coordinated—shows dexterity, agility, flexibility, balance, and poise
- Task Oriented—strives to learn by doing

Students with a strong kinesthetic intelligence:

- Seek to interact with their environment
- Enjoy hands-on activities
- Can remain focused on a hands-on task for an extended period of time
- May demonstrate strong fine and/or gross motor ability
- Prefer learning centers to seat work
- Seek out other students who are physically gregarious

- Master a principle once they can manipulate materials that demonstrate the concept
- Enjoy group games and active learning tasks
- Are different from children who are hyperactive

Teachers support this intelligence in the classroom by:

- Providing hands-on learning centers
- Incorporating creative drama into instruction
- Including interactive games in reviewing and remediating content
- Offering experiences in movement to rhythm and music
- Engaging students in hands-on science experiments
- Using manipulatives in math instruction
- Allowing opportunities for building and taking apart
- Encouraging students to construct physical representations of concepts
- Keeping students physically moving throughout the school day

Instructional technologies that stimulate this intelligence include:

- Construction tools
- Kitchen utensils
- Screw
- Lever
- Wheel and axle
- Inclined plane
- Pulley
- Wedge
- Physical education equipment

- Manipulative materials
- Mouse
- Joystick
- Simulations that require eye-hand coordination
- Assistive technologies
- Digital probes

Interpersonal Intelligence

The interpersonal intelligence promotes active learning by encouraging learners to serve as partners in knowledge-building.

Core Characteristics:

- Collaborative Skills—the capability to jointly complete tasks with others
- Cooperative Attitude—the willingness to offer and accept input
- Leadership—recognition by peers as someone to follow
- Social Influence—an ability to persuade others
- Social Empathy—an awareness and concern for others
- Social Connection—a skill for meaningfully relating to others

Students with a strong interpersonal intelligence:

- Seek the support of a group
- Value relationships
- Enjoy collaborative work
- Solicit input from others

- Enjoy sharing about themselves
- Display a "winning" personality
- Tend to be natural leaders

Teachers support this intelligence in the classroom by:
- Allowing interaction among students during learning tasks
- Including activities where students work in groups
- Providing opportunities for students to select their own groups
- Forming cooperative groups wherein each member has an assigned role
- Planning activities where students form teams to be successful
- Allowing competition that promotes higher level achievement
- Incorporating structured dramatic activities in which students can role play
- Using resource people to invigorate the classroom
- Promoting interaction with other classes by participating in learning tasks together

Instructional technologies that stimulate this intelligence include:
- Class discussion
- Sticky notes
- Greeting cards
- Laboratory
- Telephone
- Walkie-talkie
- Intercom

- Board games
- Costumes
- Collaborative projects
- Social media sites
- Message boards
- Instant messenger
- Video chat (such as Skype)

Application of the Interactive Domain

Consider five-year-old Kevin in his kindergarten classroom. He not only uses language to demonstrate his knowledge or express his needs, he also uses language to explore, inquire, and prompt responses from others. This can include the use of nonsensical expressions, repetitive recountings of favorite books, and even reverting to "baby talk." Regardless of the many functions of language Kevin is using, he consistently makes use of talk to interact with others and his environment.

Eleven-year-old Rhonda is a prime example of the interactive function of the interpersonal intelligence. As her class reads E.G. Speare's *The Witch of Blackbird Pond* she continually prompts her teacher to ask about the mores of 17th-century New England. Rhonda initiates class discussion on the social dynamics of prosecuting witches in Colonial New England, not for the sake of the discussion itself but to help her better understand the plot and setting of the story. When it comes time to be assessed for comprehension of the novel, Rhonda excels in an interview format, in which she can discuss her understandings and ideas at length. In fact, her teacher is offering several assessment options, including the opportunity to be interviewed by a class-mate as the heroine from the book.

Finally, consider Keana's use of her kinesthetic intelligence as an interactive process. Keana has been learning about electrical circuits in her third grade class. This week the teacher has set up an experiment at a learning center where Keana and her classmates must use batteries, copper wiring, and light bulbs to create electrical circuits. Keana and her group quickly create a complete circuit. They then ask their teacher for some paper clips so they can experiment with making a switch that will open and close the circuit. Finally, Keana and her group take the experiment a step further by creating a parallel circuit using two light bulbs. Keana has repeatedly interacted with her environment and her peers to create a greater understanding of how electrical circuits work.

reflection

1. How are the interactive intelligences supported in your instructional repertoire?

2. Why is the kinesthetic intelligence not more prominent in secondary education?

3. How is the interpersonal intelligence being emphasized in the Information Age?

4. In what ways can the kinesthetic and interpersonal intelligences add new dynamics in the way the linguistic intelligence is accommodated?

CHAPTER 5

the
IQuest framework

The IQuest framework takes a standard, single-minded activity and expands it across the intelligences, incorporating technology as it challenges students to think and produce at higher levels. Simple to design and use, it expands a teacher's instructional repertoire to make use of all three intelligence domains at a much higher level of thinking to create dynamic, MI-infused learning experiences.

The IQuest framework consists of three components:

Event: a facilitating activity that defines the goal for the IQuest

Process: a task that immerses students in information and/ or experience that helps them to define the product they are working to create or the problem they are trying to solve

Performance: the culmination of the quest, in which students display and demonstrate their learning

Each component of the IQuest targets one intelligence domain. This means there are six different ways that the event, process, and performance can combine with the three domains to create MI-infused learning experiences. By referring to these IQuest types when planning for instruction, teachers can plan lessons and units that effectively address all of the intelligences in the classroom. These six types of IQuests are explained further in the next section.

To craft an IQuest, the teacher first needs to identify the overall learning objective. The instructional experience they are developing should meet that objective. Based on the objective, the teacher would then select one of the six IQuest models (detailed in Chapters 6–11) and, using the appropriate template, plug in the specific target intelligence(s). From there the teacher would strategically formulate tasks that map to the identified intelligences, selecting strategies and technologies that will support students so that they can successfully learn the intended objective. Each of the examples in this book will help illustrate the possibilities for the IQuest in your own instructional repertoire.

IQuests can be developed using existing instructional plans or built from the ground up as original projects. When building from existing lessons, first identify those intelligences that are already being addressed and where they fit into the framework. Then add the intelligences that you will target to make the learning experience more powerful for students. When creating an IQuest from scratch, target one of the six models in this book and build instruction that stimulates the intelligences in that model.

The Six Types of IQuests

These six ways of looking at building IQuests into instruction will help teachers get a better handle on all of the intelligences while expanding their instructional repertoire. We will explore each of these types in the following chapters. Using these types as presented is a good way to start using IQuests, but with experience and confidence teachers can modify these six types in new and innovative ways as they see new possibilities for instruction.

Evaluation Exchange IQuest (see Chapter 6)

Objective: Delivering data meaningfully

Event: Analytic domain

Process: Introspective domain

Performance: Interactive domain

Critical Collaboration IQuest (see Chapter 7)

Objective: Working to build consensus

Event: Analytic domain

Process: Interactive domain

Performance: Introspective domain

Partner Puzzle IQuest (see Chapter 8)

Objective: Authentic problem solving

Event: Interactive domain

Process: Analytic domain

Performance: Introspective domain

People Perspective IQuest (see Chapter 9)

Objective: Seeing multiple solutions

Event: Interactive domain

Process: Introspective domain

Performance: Analytic domain

Qualitative Quantities IQuest (see Chapter 10)

Objective: Creating products in context

Event: Introspective domain

Process: Analytic domain

Performance: Interactive domain

Principle Partners IQuest (see Chapter 11)

Objective: Information literacy meets cultural literacy

Event: Introspective domain

Process: Interactive domain

Performance: Analytic domain

Applying the IQuest Format to Worksheets, Lessons, and Projects

The simple IQuest format can have powerful implications for instruction, from worksheets to lessons to projects. Let's examine an example of each.

Worksheet

This is an example of how I turned a simple, problem-solving worksheet into an IQuest. I started with the Canine Calories worksheet (Figure 5.1), which asks students to calculate the calories needed for sled dogs to run the length of a trail. Traditionally this would be an individual seat assignment requiring about twenty minutes and a finite set of computation skills. However, this type of activity can easily be expanded to accommodate all the intelligence domains by applying the IQuest framework.

Canine Calories

Dogs need a lot of energy while pulling a sled along the trail. They burn lots of calories!

1. If each dog burns up about 7,000 calories of food a day pulling a sled, how many calories does a team of 12 dogs burn in a day?

2. If a hamburger is 200 calories, how many burgers would each dog have to eat in order to get their 7,000 calories for a day?

3. Your pet dog at home uses one-fifth the calories of a sled dog. How many calories does your dog burn up a day?

4. The human diet is about 1,500 calories a day. How many humans could a full day of sled dog calories feed?

5. If a sled dog burns 7,000 calories a day and it takes nine days to complete the trail, how many calories will that dog have consumed by the end of the journey?

Figure 5.1 Canine Calories worksheet

In this case, the worksheet's format dictated the domain assigned to the process; this IQuest will have an analytic (problem solving) process. I determined that this IQuest should also have problem solving as its learning objective and that this should be a Partner Puzzle IQuest. This meant that the intelligence domain for the event would be interactive and the introspective domain would be covered in the performance.

Zooming in on the event's interactive domain, I decided to focus on the kinesthetic intelligence by having students work together as a team to pull a sled (or simulated mass) so that they could experience the work of sled dogs. This would give them a conceptual point of reference for completing the Canine Calories worksheet, which is dominated by the logical intelligence (completing word problems).

For the performance task, I decided to target the intrapersonal intelligence. Students would be asked to determine the number of calories needed for the dog team they will follow in the Iditarod sled dog race, emailing the team mushers to share their recommendations.

The following is how this would look using the IQuest framework.

Partner Puzzle IQuest **Canine Calories**	
EVENT	
Domain	Interactive
Intelligence(s)	Kinesthetic
Task	Students pull a dogsled as a team.
PROCESS	
Domain	Analytic
Intelligence(s)	Logical
Task	Complete Canine Calories worksheet.
PERFORMANCE	
Domain	Introspective
Intelligence(s)	Intrapersonal
Task	Determine calorie recommendations for Iditarod sled team.

From this example you can see how the IQuest format takes a standard, single-minded activity and expands it across the intelligences, incorporating technology as it challenges students to think and produce at higher levels. Consider the higher level of understanding students would have about calorie intake after completing this IQuest!

Lesson

Let's take a look at a second application of the IQuest, the traditional lesson. In this example students are asked to design a complex machine, based on their study of simple machines. When using the IQuest with a lesson, start by identifying the event domain. In this example I selected the introspective domain for the event, encouraging student reflection and planning prior to actually beginning their design work.

Next, consider the performance task, making sure the outcome of your student work aligns nicely with the event. The performance task should reflect your lesson objective, so in this case I selected the analytic domain. This leaves the interactive domain for the process. The IQuest type is Principle Partners.

Let's break it down further. In the event, students brainstorm the criteria for a successful complex machine. The intelligences involved are the intrapersonal (feelings and values) and the existential (the connection to the larger world around us, in this case prospective buyers of our machine).

For the process, students will work in teams using CAD software to design an original machine based on the criteria they have identified. The intelligences accommodated are the interpersonal (working with others) and kinesthetic (working with models, fine motor skills).

For the performance students will evaluate each team's machine design against the criteria agreed upon at the beginning of the lesson. This will involve the logical (critical thinking) and naturalist (classifying and categorizing) intelligences.

Principle Partners IQuest **Designing a complex machine**	
EVENT	
Domain	Introspective
Intelligence(s)	Intrapersonal, Existential
Task	Identify criteria for successful complex machines.
PROCESS	
Domain	Interactive
Intelligence(s)	Interpersonal, Kinesthetic
Task	Design complex machines based on criteria.
PERFORMANCE	
Domain	Analytic
Intelligence(s)	Logical, Naturalist
Task	Evaluate complex machines against the established criteria.

Again, the IQuest format stretches the teacher's planning to make use of all three intelligence domains at a much higher level of thinking, while involving technology.

Project

As a final example let's consider an IQuest project. In a project, it's important to begin with the performance outcome because a project (by definition) is activity and product based. In the following Art and Architecture project, the performance outcome is introspective, evaluating structures to identify the best examples of local architecture. The process domain is identified second. In this project the process is analytic, as students sort and rank images. This leaves the interactive domain for the facilitating event of the project. This is a Partner Puzzle IQuest.

In the facilitating event, students work in teams to take field trips in their community and photograph examples of architecture from different neighborhoods and business districts. This involves all the intelligences in the domain—linguistic, interpersonal, and kinesthetic.

In the process phase, students classify, categorize, identify patterns in, and analyze the examples of architecture to determine which are the best examples of their community's heritage and history. This uses the logical, rhythmic, and naturalist intelligences.

And finally, in the performance phase of this project IQuest, students create a multimedia presentation that celebrates the architecture of their town, showcasing examples that exemplify their community's history, culture, and values. The creation of the presentation calls on spatial, existential, and intrapersonal intelligences.

Note how each domain is fully stimulated by a project: all three intelligences in each domain are accommodated. This is a much stronger use of the intelligences than worksheets or traditional lessons.

Here is the project in the IQuest format.

Partner Puzzle IQuest	
Arts and Architecture Project	
EVENT	
Domain	Interactive
Intelligence(s)	Linguistic, Interpersonal, Kinesthetic
Task	Take a field trip to view, discuss, and photograph local architecture.
PROCESS	
Domain	Analytic
Intelligence(s)	Logical, Rhythmic, Naturalist
Task	Classify, categorize [identify patterns], and rank photographic images.
PERFORMANCE	
Domain	Introspective
Intelligence(s)	Spatial, Existential, Intrapersonal
Task	Create a multimedia presentation of the best examples of local architecture.

Targeting Intelligences

Once you have selected a domain for each IQuest component, you must decide which intelligence(s) within each domain to target. There are two ways to approach this: balancing intelligences and strengthening intelligences.

Balancing Intelligences

In planning a lesson, a teacher may wish to select one intelligence from each domain in order to provide for a well-balanced accommodation of the intelligences.

For example, Mrs. Chin has a lesson on iambic pentameter in which, given a sonnet, the learner will recite the sonnet with proper meter and interpretation of its content. This lesson may benefit from using the verbal (interactive), rhythmic (analytic), and existential (introspective) intelligences. By tapping into all three of these ways of knowing she can accommodate learners across the spectrum in her classroom.

If you put the lesson into the IQuest format, it might look something like this:

Partner Puzzle IQuest **Reciting a Sonnet**	
EVENT	
Domain	Interactive
Intelligence(s)	Linguistic
Task	Recite the sonnet.
PROCESS	
Domain	Analytic
Intelligence(s)	Rhythmic
Task	Experience the sonnet's meter through repeated practice sessions.
PERFORMANCE	
Domain	Introspective
Intelligence(s)	Existential
Task	Interpret the sentiment expressed in the sonnet.

Strengthening Intelligences

In planning instruction for learners, a teacher may wish to target all the intelligences of a specific domain to provide experiences that strengthen that particular domain.

For example, Mr. Bergman realizes that his students need to improve their critical thinking skills in order to be prepared for upcoming standardized testing in biology. To achieve this, he wants to emphasize the analytical nature of his Dissecting an Earthworm lesson. So, for the process he decides to map to all three—logical, rhythmic, and naturalist—analytic intelligences. The objective of the lesson is for the learner to follow instructions to dissect an earthworm, categorizing organs by body systems and identifying patterns found within those systems.

The process portion of the the lesson in the IQuest format might look like the following.

IQuest **Dissecting an Earthworm**	
EVENT	
Domain	
Intelligence(s)	
Tasks	
PROCESS	
Domain	Analytic
Intelligence(s)	Logical, Rhythmic, Naturalist
Tasks	Follow body systems throughout the organism. (Logical) Identify patterns within and between body systems. (Rhythmic) Categorize organs and body systems by function. (Naturalist)

PERFORMANCE	
Domain	
Intelligence(s)	
Tasks	

reflection

1. Which IQuest types are best suited to your instructional style?

2. Which topics in your curriculum are potentially rich for IQuest development?

3. Are problem solving and product making mutually exclusive IQuest goals?

4. Examine an existing lesson against the three intelligence domains. Which domains are well supported in your lesson? Which domains need to be better incorporated?

the
evaluation exchange
IQuest
Delivering Data Meaningfully

I n the 21st-century workplace, information is the coin of the realm, but information is not an end unto itself. One of the major goals is not only interpretation of information, but also delivery of that information to the end-user in pertinent, meaningful ways. This requires the ability to analyze data as well as place it in contexts that provide insight and perspective. The Evaluation Exchange IQuest gives learners opportunities to work through this process in a variety of ways across the curriculum.

Structure

Analytic Event. The event facilitates the lesson by launching students on a mission to create a product or solve a problem through an authentic task. Using the analytic domain, participants in this IQuest will work to identify patterns, organize data, and/or logically form a conclusion based on the data presented. This is not a goal in and of itself, but a precipitating event that sets the stage for the real work of this IQuest, the process.

Introspective Process. Using the introspective domain, participants take the data from the event and make sense of it through their own feelings, values, and attitudes; through connections to larger truths; and through visual representation. Once this phase is complete, the process concludes with the performance.

Interactive Performance. The interactive domain provides the stage for presenting the findings of the IQuest: the analyzed data within the context of the introspective process. This can culminate in a variety of ways depending on the objectives of the IQuest.

The structure, in template format, for an Evaluation Exchange IQuest is shown on the next page.

Evaluation Exchange IQuest **Delivering Data Meaningfully**	
EVENT	
Domain	Analytic
Intelligence(s)	Logical, Rhythmic, Naturalist
Task	Interpret data for pattern, order, and reason.
PROCESS	
Domain	Introspective
Intelligence(s)	Intrapersonal, Existential, Spatial
Task	Examine personal, communal, and spatial implications.
PERFORMANCE	
Domain	Interactive
Intelligence(s)	Interpersonal, Kinesthetic, Linguistic
Task	Share resulting understanding through interaction.

Example

Let's look at an example of an Evaluation Exchange IQuest on global pandemics. As the world continues to shrink through advances in communication and transportation, the likelihood of disease (such as avian flu) spreading worldwide becomes more and more likely as carriers travel from continent to continent. Assessing the implications of such a catastrophic event is a real world application of understanding in which there may be multiple solutions to the problem.

Evaluation Exchange IQuest
Global Pandemics

EVENT	
Domain	Analytic
Intelligence(s)	Logical, Rhythmic, Naturalist
Tasks	Students examine and collect data on the spread of avian flu throughout the world:
	• Global Initiative on Sharing Avian Influenza Data: *http://platform.gisaid.org/epi3/frontend*
	• Google Earth maps of avian flu spread: *http://declanbutler.info/Flumaps1/avianflu.html*
	• World Health Organization: Influenza at the Human–Animal Interface: *www.who.int/influenza/human_animal_interface/*
	Students place data in an organizer that helps put it in context: spreadsheet, database, semantic map.
	Students identify common patterns, themes, classifications, categories, hierarchies, or any other schematic system that helps to make sense of the information collected.
PROCESS	
Domain	Introspective
Intelligence(s)	Intrapersonal, Existential, Spatial
Tasks	Students use individual blogs to develop their ideas on how to handle a pandemic in their community. Students address the following questions.
	• How would disease spread in an outbreak?
	• Who is most susceptible?
	• Who should be the priority for protection?
	• How should the community respond?
	Read and respond to each student blog as ideas develop over time.

PERFORMANCE	
Domain	Interactive
Intelligence(s)	Interpersonal, Linguistic
Tasks	Students build a wiki that relates class findings, priorities, and recommendations for the impact of a pandemic in the community.
	Post the wiki online and link to it from your class website. Invite others outside your classroom to contribute to the wiki. Have students review and edit the wiki as it is modified over time.

Characteristics

Notice the characteristics of this IQuest:

1. The activities map to all three intelligence domains.

2. Students are allowed to encounter the data sources in an open-ended manner. They are not instructed how to make sense of the information.

3. Blogging is used as a tool for personal reflection.

4. Teacher interaction in individual blogs is critical for the development of student ideas.

5. The culmination of each student blog should be a summary of that student's convictions and conclusions.

6. The wiki must be set up and ready for students to use before the performance section of the IQuest.

7. The IQuest does not conclude with the posting of student input on the wiki. Student editing of outside posts to the wiki takes student performance to the highest levels of Bloom's taxonomy.

8. The end product of the IQuest is a quality online presence that shares information and ideas and evolves over time in the future.

Of course, depending on the location of your community, responses to a pandemic will differ. Solutions to real-world problems are culturally based. Authentic tasks framed in an IQuest are open to cultural interpretations. There will be more than one correct answer.

In an Evaluation Exchange IQuest, answers change with the data analyzed. At first students may be inclined to react to a pandemic outbreak based on the data from the initial outbreak in Vietnam. However, by studying additional information from Thailand, China, and Canada they gain a broader perspective of how the disease spreads and how communities respond.

Most importantly, an Evaluation Exchange IQuest emphasizes the communal nature of data. In real-world problem solving there's not only more than one correct answer, students can gain depth perception by gathering information and ideas from multiple sources. In fact, the nature of communal information is that the truth is sifted out through a process of rigorous inter-action; since there is no one central authority purveying truth, it is determined over time by the interaction of ideas proffered by a diverse population of contributors.

The Evaluation Exchange IQuest engages students in a prac-tical exercise of data gathering and analysis that is relevant and meaningful in today's world. In the 21st-century work-place, workers must be able to employ these skills to solve the complex problems of our shrinking global community.

Correlation to the ISTE NETS for Students

This IQuest maps to all six standards:

1. Creativity and Innovation

Students demonstrate creative thinking, construct knowledge, and develop innovative products and processes using technology. Students:

d. identify trends and forecast possibilities

2. Communication and Collaboration

Students use digital media and environments to communicate and work collaboratively, including at a distance, to support individual learning and contribute to the learning of others. Students:

a. interact, collaborate, and publish with peers, experts, or others employing a variety of digital environments and media

3. Research and Information Fluency

Students apply digital tools to gather, evaluate, and use information. Students:

a. plan strategies to guide inquiry

b. locate, organize, analyze, evaluate, synthesize, and ethically use information from a variety of sources and media

d. process data and report results

4. Critical Thinking, Problem Solving, and Decision Making

Students use critical thinking skills to plan and conduct research, manage projects, solve problems, and make

informed decisions using appropriate digital tools and resources. Students:

    c. collect and analyze data to identify solutions and/or make informed decisions

5. Digital Citizenship

Students understand human, cultural, and societal issues related to technology and practice legal and ethical behavior. Students:

    a. advocate and practice safe, legal, and responsible use of information and technology

6. Technology Operations and Concepts

Students demonstrate a sound understanding of technology concepts, systems, and operations. Students:

    a. understand and use technology systems

reflection

1. How does the Evaluation Exchange IQuest place the focus on meaningful use of data?

2. How does the wiki support the goals of the Evaluation Exchange IQuest?

3. What are the pros and cons of building understandings as a community?

4. What other technologies would be appropriate to use in an Evaluation Exchange IQuest?

the
critical collaboration
IQuest
Working to Build Consensus

B eyond the skills of information literacy, the ability to collaborate online with partners from disparate geographic locations is key in the Information Age workplace. The Critical Collaboration IQuest places the emphasis squarely on this ability to not only collaborate but build consensus among colleagues.

Structure

Analytic Event. The analytic event compels students to solve a problem or create a product based on a real-world need. This can be done through a facilitating experience or the presentation of compelling data. Regardless of the impetus, the event should launch students into a mission with an identified objective in mind.

Interactive Process. The interactive process engages students to make sense of the presenting event so that they can successfully achieve their objective. This can be done through written and oral discussion, virtual and real-world interaction, and manipulation of objects and data that help to clarify understanding of the subject being studied.

Introspective Performance. The introspective domain provides the stage for placing value on the understanding students have achieved through the process. It is through being able to see the value of what is known—to appreciate its impact on the larger community and to assimilate it into our own feelings, values, and attitudes—that we truly master new information, skills, and concepts.

The structure, in template format, for a Critical Collaboration IQuest is on the next page.

Critical Collaboration IQuest **Working to Build Consensus**	
EVENT	
Domain	Analytic
Intelligence(s)	Logical, Rhythmic, Naturalist
Task	Interpret data or experience for pattern, order, and reason.
PROCESS	
Domain	Interactive
Intelligence(s)	Interpersonal, Kinesthetic, Linguistic
Task	Interact with others and the environment to broaden understanding.
PERFORMANCE	
Domain	Introspective
Intelligence(s)	Intrapersonal, Existential, Spatial
Task	Assign value to the new understanding acquired.

Example

Consider this Critical Collaboration IQuest on digital currency. As web-based services continue to expand, it will become more and more necessary to be able to use a currency small enough to pay for information by the byte or kilobyte, rather than by our traditional measurements for paying for goods and services. Determining the parameters for such a currency and developing a proposal for consideration in digital commerce is a practical extension of many skills already embedded in the curriculum.

Critical Collaboration IQuest
Digital Currency

EVENT	
Domain	Analytic
Intelligence(s)	Logical, Rhythmic, Naturalist
Tasks	Students survey the current cost for information services online: • What units of measurement are currently used to sell digital information? • What does that cost breakdown to in cost per megabyte? Kilobyte? Byte? • What kind of currency would need to be developed to fairly assess fees for byte-sized pieces of information sold online? • How would that payment be made over the Internet? Students use a spreadsheet to break down costs using formulae and auto-fill features. Students identify standard units and costs for different sizes of digital information. Students create a semantic map of currency suggestions.
PROCESS	
Domain	Interactive
Intelligence(s)	Interpersonal, Kinesthetic, Linguistic
Tasks	Students meet with partners from other schools in a collaborative multiuser virtual environment in real time, to examine and discuss findings and proposals. This should be done in multiple online work sessions over time. Each session should build on the previous one and work towards consensus on a proposed digital currency.

PERFORMANCE	
Domain	Introspective
Intelligence(s)	Intrapersonal, Existential
Tasks	Students work together to create an image that represents the proposed digital currency.
	Students use spreadsheet data and online collaborative findings to make a case for the proposed currency.
	Students create a multimedia presentation that can be posted on the web that explains the proposed currency, its value per bytes, kilobytes and beyond, and the method through which online purchasers of information can acquire and spend this currency.

Characteristics

Notice the characteristics of this IQuest:

1. The activities map to all three intelligence domains.

2. Students are allowed to encounter the data from a variety of commerce sources online.

3. Spreadsheet functions are an excellent tool for disaggregating data.

4. Students are asked to collaborate with students from other geographic locations outside of their own classroom and/or school.

5. The use of a multiuser virtual environment is key in online collaboration.

6. The process of online collaboration is an excellent opportunity to sharpen virtual facilitation skills absent the nonverbal cues of face-to-face interaction.

7. The culmination of online collaboration should be a consensus on what the final work product should be.

8. Findings should be delivered via the web.

The key to online collaboration is making use of a virtual environment appropriate to your learners and the task you have given them. For a text-based multiuser virtual environment (MUVE), consider Tapped In (http://tappedin.org), an online community of professional educators that provides a safe environment conducive to collaboration. Set up like a virtual campus, Tapped In offers the ability to host live virtual events and record a transcript of what took place, which is then emailed to you once you log out.

Of particular value in Tapped In is the Student Activities Center, where students can log in under a teacher's account and work in a structured work area with peers. There are actually six "rooms" in the SAC where students can work in small groups without disturbing one another, and each room records its own transcript of discussion, freeing the teacher to circulate among the groups virtually. When the session is over and students log out, the transcript of each group's session is emailed to the teacher.

Another great technology for collaborating online is Skype (www.skype.com), a free Internet telephony service that can provide for group phone discussion without the restrictions of a text-based environment. Skype can utilize both voice and video, requiring users to practice good netiquette—and learn to take turns and listen well—while interacting in real-time online.

The Critical Collaboration IQuest puts the emphasis on people in making productive use of critical thinking. Students may have great ideas, but they must know how to communicate them and build consensus for those ideas among colleagues in the Information Age workplace.

Correlation to the ISTE NETS for Students

This IQuest maps to all six standards:

1. Creativity and Innovation

Students demonstrate creative thinking, construct knowledge, and develop innovative products and processes using technology. Students:

    c. use models and simulations to explore complex systems and issues

2. Communication and Collaboration

Students use digital media and environments to communicate and work collaboratively, including at a distance, to support individual learning and contribute to the learning of others. Students:

    d. contribute to project teams to produce original works or solve problems

3. Research and Information Fluency

Students apply digital tools to gather, evaluate, and use information. Students:

    a. plan strategies to guide inquiry

    b. locate, organize, analyze, evaluate, synthesize, and ethically use information from a variety of sources and media

    d. process data and report results

4. Critical Thinking, Problem Solving, and Decision Making

Students use critical thinking skills to plan and conduct research, manage projects, solve problems, and make

informed decisions using appropriate digital tools and resources. Students:

a. identify and define authentic problems and significant questions for investigation

5. Digital Citizenship

Students understand human, cultural, and societal issues related to technology and practice legal and ethical behavior. Students:

d. exhibit leadership for digital citizenship

6. Technology Operations and Concepts

Students demonstrate a sound understanding of technology concepts, systems, and operations. Students:

d. transfer current knowledge to learning of new technologies

reflection

1. How does the Critical Collaboration IQuest make information literacy an active process?

2. When is it better to work in a virtual environment? Face to face?

3. How can a data file be shared and modified between partners in a virtual environment?

4. What other real world tasks may be suitable for a Critical Collaboration IQuest?

CHAPTER 8

the partner puzzle IQuest
Authentic Problem Solving

Technology's ability to break down the classroom barriers of time and space opens up the entire world to your students. There is nothing like a real-time event to fill learners with excitement and wonder. The Partner Puzzle IQuest capitalizes on this unique capability.

Structure

Interactive Event. The event is an interactive activity that helps students make a connection with the real world. It can be any event that is displayed publicly, from a tournament to a race, an election to the Olympics. By following such an event online as a group, students will discover a spontaneous sense of excitement and a shared investment in learning. Richer in content than a simulation, the Partner Puzzle IQuest is the ultimate authentic task.

Analytic Process. The process maps to the analytic domain of intelligences, requiring students to analyze information they have gathered in the IQuest event. This can include critical analysis of the event, the disaggregation of data, and the identification of patterns and categories of event-related information.

Introspective Performance. The introspective performance takes the detached analysis of data and personalizes it so that students can internalize understanding and relate it to their existing knowledge base. Real-time, affective events add an emotional component to learning that cannot be replicated in artificial or contrived methods of teaching and learning. The Partner Puzzle IQuest format is synonymous with authentic learning.

The structure, in template format, for a Partner Puzzle IQuest is on the next page.

Partner Puzzle IQuest **Authentic Problem Solving**	
EVENT	
Domain	Interactive
Intelligence(s)	Interpersonal, Kinesthetic, Linguistic
Task	Experience a real-time event online.
PROCESS	
Domain	Analytic
Intelligence(s)	Logical, Rhythmic, Naturalist
Task	Assess the real-time event and/or data collected from it.
PERFORMANCE	
Domain	Introspective
Intelligence(s)	Intrapersonal, Existential, Spatial
Task	Personalize the real-time experience to extend learning.

Example

Consider this Partner Puzzle IQuest on a presidential election. National elections such as a run for the presidency are rich with data, drama, and opportunities for problem solving. From an awareness of local political tradition to a study of voting trends and an examination of the candidates' stands on the issues, the experience is full of possibilities, culminating with an online election that compares student voting results with those of the electorate.

Partner Puzzle IQuest
Presidential Election

EVENT	
Domain	Interactive
Intelligence(s)	Interpersonal, Linguistic
Tasks	Conduct an online roll call of the states that invites students from each state to share their preferences on the major presidential candidates and their stands on the issues.
	Ask each responding class to identify its state, its class choice for President, and its stand on the major issues of the campaign.
	Have your students recognize each participating class and share their vote and views for your home state.
	Ideally there is at least one class representing each state. There can be more than one class from each state.

PROCESS	
Domain	Analytic
Intelligence(s)	Logical, Rhythmic, Naturalist
Tasks	Students tally the votes of each state represented in the roll call. In the event that more than one class represents a state, the data can be averaged.
	Students sort and classify each state's stand on the major issues of the election.

PERFORMANCE	
Domain	Introspective
Intelligence(s)	Intrapersonal, Existential, Spatial
Tasks	Students identify the campaign issues that are the determining factors in the results of your roll call vote.
	Students determine who should win the election, based on popular vote of your roll call and on the electoral votes of each state.
	Students create graphs that show the roll call results by popular and electoral vote.
	Students deliver a web presentation of your class's findings that can be shared with participating classes in your roll call.
	Compare your roll call results with the results of the actual election.

Characteristics

Notice the characteristics of this IQuest:

1. A blog is an excellent asynchronous tool that allows students to connect to a real-time event across class schedules and time zones.

2. Google Docs can be used to tally the collection of data contributed by classes from different areas of the country.

3. Data collected is both qualitative and quantitative in nature.

4. Data can be placed in a database or spreadsheet to help identify patterns and trends.

5. Stands on issues can be sorted in a table or other graphic organizer.

6. The performance allows for both a reflection on one's personal values and the collective values of society.

7. Graphic representation of data can be an extension of information entered into spreadsheets.

8. Findings can be delivered via the web so that other classes can benefit from your students' work.

Planning for a Partner Puzzle IQuest requires advance preparation to align your class's work with the real-time event. If a national election takes place in November, the roll call should be held in September so there is time to analyze data and report your class findings in October.

For a sporting event such as the Olympics or the NCAA basketball tournament, planning should be done several months in advance so that you can research the best resources online for immersing your students in the experience. In the case of the Olympics, students may plan a travel itinerary using travel agent pricing, and then keep medal counts for participating nations. For March Madness, students can create graphic organizers of the results of each round.

Consider following the Iditarod Trail Sled Dog Race or Tour de France as a Partner Puzzle IQuest. Students can follow a team throughout the race, evaluate elapsed time and strategies, and assess the success of the team at the conclusion of the race.

The Partner Puzzle IQuest motivates students to participate at a high level of Bloom's taxonomy, actively creating and evaluating information to facilitate meaningful construction of understanding.

Correlation to the
ISTE NETS for Students

This IQuest maps to all six standards:

1. Creativity and Innovation

Students demonstrate creative thinking, construct knowledge, and develop innovative products and processes using technology. Students:

b. create original works as a means of personal or group expression

2. Communication and Collaboration

Students use digital media and environments to communicate and work collaboratively, including at a distance, to support individual learning and contribute to the learning of others. Students:

c. develop cultural understanding and global awareness by engaging with learners of other cultures

3. Research and Information Fluency

Students apply digital tools to gather, evaluate, and use information. Students:

c. evaluate and select information sources and digital tools based on the appropriateness to specific tasks

d. process data and report results

4. Critical Thinking, Problem Solving, and Decision Making

Students use critical thinking skills to plan and conduct research, manage projects, solve problems, and make informed decisions using appropriate digital tools and resources. Students:

    b. plan and manage activities to develop a solution or complete a project

5. Digital Citizenship

Students understand human, cultural, and societal issues related to technology and practice legal and ethical behavior. Students:

    b. exhibit a positive attitude toward using technology that supports collaboration, learning, and productivity

6. Technology Operations and Concepts

Students demonstrate a sound understanding of technology concepts, systems, and operations. Students:

    b. select and use applications effectively and productively

reflection

1. Could you design a Partner Puzzle IQuest that does not involve a real-time event?

2. How far in advance would you need to plan to recruit classes from outside your area to participate in your Partner Puzzle IQuest project?

3. Which technologies are best suited for experiencing real-time events?

4. What upcoming real-time events might be suitable for a Partner Puzzle IQuest for your students?

the
people perspective
IQuest
Seeing Multiple Solutions

I n the Information Age, the ability to look at a problem from multiple points of view and generate varied solutions is critical. One of the challenges of teaching information literacy is to help students develop strategies to gather information from multiple sources rather than accepting one source as a definitive. The People Perspective IQuest facilitates this by challenging students to identify multiple solutions to a problem. The culminating task is to select the solution that best addresses the need as defined within a community.

Structure

Interactive Event. The interactive event is an engaging activity that serves as an impetus for further investigation. This can be an immersion in data, a real-world experience, or participation in a classroom activity that leads students to identify a problem they need to address. A well-designed interactive event will inspire students to want to dig deeper, discover answers, and find resolution for the identified problem.

Introspective Process. The introspective process affords students the opportunity to filter the IQuest event through their own feelings, values, and attitudes and to explore the impact that the problem (and a possible solution) has on their school and/or the larger community. A constructivist approach to this would be identifying criteria for evaluating solutions to a problem before actually exploring possible solutions. These criteria can be placed in a rubric to help quantify solutions in the performance phase of the IQuest.

Analytic Performance. The analytic performance charges the students to identify and evaluate possible solutions to the problem presented. Involving students in cooperative groups within the classroom or from multiple schools or classrooms ensures a rigorous process of investigation and evaluation. The result of an effective People Perspective IQuest is a rich set of possible solutions prioritized against the criteria set up during the process portion of the activity.

The structure, in template format, for a People Perspective IQuest is shown on the next page.

People Perspective IQuest **Seeing Multiple Solutions**	
EVENT	
Domain	Interactive
Intelligence(s)	Interpersonal, Kinesthetic, Linguistic
Task	Engage in immersive experience, activity, or data exploration that necessitates the search for a solution to an identified problem.
PROCESS	
Domain	Introspective
Intelligence(s)	Intrapersonal, Existential, Spatial
Task	Craft criteria that reflect personal and communal values.
PERFORMANCE	
Domain	Analytic
Intelligence(s)	Logical, Rhythmic, Naturalist
Task	Generate and rank possible solutions.

Example

Consider this People Perspective IQuest on alternative fuels. In this century the need for energy options will continue to play a major role scientifically, politically, and domestically. Challenging students to consider society's options for alternative fuels is an authentic, contemporary concern in which the ramifications of different solutions need to be considered carefully.

People Perspective IQuest
Alternative Fuels

EVENT

Domain	Interactive
Intelligence(s)	Interpersonal, Linguistic
Tasks	Present the Energy Policy Act of 2005 (www1.eere. energy.gov/femp/regulations/epact2005.html) and have students examine and discuss it in cooperative groups.
	Have groups generate a list of alternative fuels that the government may want to consider in carrying out the Energy Policy Act.
	Bring groups together and compile a master list of alternative fuel options.

PROCESS

Domain	Introspective
Intelligence(s)	Intrapersonal, Existential, Spatial
Tasks	Cooperative groups work to identify personal and communal values that should be considered in evaluating alternative fuels.
	Have groups generate a list of criteria for evaluating alternative fuels based on personal and communal values.
	Bring the groups together and compile a comprehensive list of criteria.
	Prioritize the criteria based on importance.
	Work as a class to develop a rubric based on the established criteria.
	Place the rubric in a spreadsheet so that the scores can autocalculate.

PERFORMANCE	
Domain	Analytic
Intelligence(s)	Logical, Rhythmic, Naturalist
Tasks	Groups research alternative fuels.
	Students evaluate findings on each fuel against the criteria placed in the evaluation rubric.
	Students prioritize alternative fuels based on rubric results.
	Students identify the best alternative fuel solution(s) based on the Energy Policy Act of 2005.

Characteristics

Notice the characteristics of this IQuest:

1. Cooperative groups can be done in the classroom or in a MUVE to connect your students with learners from disparate geographical locations.

2. Generation of a list of alternative fuel types can be done through a variety of brainstorming ideas.

3. Identifying values and criteria are subjective processes. Be inclusive and do not reject any suggestion out of hand.

4. When the entire group comes together to create a comprehensive list of criteria, each suggestion can be discussed and included or discarded based on group consensus.

5. Prioritizing criteria should be done through whole group discussion and consensus.

6. Placing prioritized criteria in a rubric requires the inclusion of exemplars that describe degrees of

proximity to the stated criterion from least to most. Each exemplar should be given a numerical value for easy quantification of rubric results.

7. Research of alternative fuels should be done using traditional and digital resources. All information should be verified by multiple reference sources.

8. The final ranking and selection of best alternative fuel options is simply the scoring of each rubric.

The People Perspective IQuest brings together collaboration and critical analysis to help students solve problems through teamwork. The key is to identify a contemporary, high-interest issue that will engage students in looking for practical, applicable solutions.

While a classroom-based People Perspective IQuest is a great way to start, the full power of this format is utilized when you bring together students from different locations around the globe. Imagine the impact of examining alternative fuel solutions through the filter of cultures from Europe, Asia, Africa, and South America. Your students would be building understandings not only about energy and problem solving, but the global-political implications for a national energy policy.

The People Perspective IQuest helps your students appreciate the human variable in any problem-solving equation. Regardless of the topic you select, this particular IQuest does an excellent job of plugging into the introspective and interactive intelligences.

Correlation to the ISTE NETS for Students:

This IQuest maps to all six standards:

1. Creativity and Innovation

Students demonstrate creative thinking, construct knowledge, and develop innovative products and processes using technology. Students:

   a. apply existing knowledge to generate new ideas, products, or processes

2. Communication and Collaboration

Students use digital media and environments to communicate and work collaboratively, including at a distance, to support individual learning and contribute to the learning of others. Students:

   d. contribute to project teams to produce original works or solve problems

3. Research and Information Fluency

Students apply digital tools to gather, evaluate, and use information. Students:

   c. evaluate and select information sources and digital tools based on the appropriateness to specific tasks

4. Critical Thinking, Problem Solving, and Decision Making

Students use critical thinking skills to plan and conduct research, manage projects, solve problems, and make informed decisions using appropriate digital tools and resources. Students:

   d. use multiple processes and diverse perspectives to explore alternative solutions

5. Digital Citizenship

Students understand human, cultural, and societal issues related to technology and practice legal and ethical behavior. Students:

c. demonstrate personal responsibility for lifelong learning

6. Technology Operations and Concepts

Students demonstrate a sound understanding of technology concepts, systems, and operations. Students:

d. transfer current knowledge to learning of new technologies

reflection

1. Are there always multiple solutions to a problem?

2. Which applications are best suited for a People Perspective IQuest?

3. Are you more likely to use a three-point rubric or a four-point rubric? Why?

4. What other topics might be suitable for a People Perspective IQuest for your students?

CHAPTER 10

the
qualitative quantities
IQuest
Creating Products in Context

O ftentimes a challenge requires us to know its context before we can decide how to act. The context can be anything from societal norms to community implications, from visual data to personal beliefs and values. And within the context of an issue there can be a variety of variables at play, from competing interests to forces of physics. Knowing all the variables in play helps to find a solution that best satisfies all the conditions for success.

Structure

Introspective Event. The introspective event allows IQuest participants to examine the needs that must be considered in their work. By tapping into students' feelings, the big picture context of a situation, and the boundless limits of their collective imagination, students can be better prepared to begin the creative process.

Analytic Process. The analytic process immerses students in the information they need to begin their work. This can include researching, identifying, analyzing, and organizing information from a variety of sources. In addition to traditional resources, students can examine primary sources, confer with content experts, and conduct original experiments that help them to gather the information they need to offer recommendations for the performance phase of the quest.

Interactive Performance. The interactive performance invites students to present their conclusions to others and offer a suggested resolution to the challenge presented in the IQuest. This can be done by acting out a scenario, presenting findings as a panel of experts, or creating a video presentation that can be posted online. In the virtual world, a well-developed website is an excellent vehicle for showcasing student work products or problem-solving solutions to a larger audience.

The structure, in template format, for a Qualitative Quantities IQuest is shown on the next page.

Qualitative Quantities IQuest		
Creating Products in Context		
EVENT		
Domain	Introspective	
Intelligence(s)	Intrapersonal, Existential, Spatial	
Task	Examine the personal and communal contexts of an issue.	
PROCESS		
Domain	Analytic	
Intelligence(s)	Logical, Rhythmic, Naturalist	
Task	Gather, analyze, and organize data.	
PERFORMANCE		
Domain	Interactive	
Intelligence(s)	Interpersonal, Kinesthetic, Linguistic	
Task	Present findings as a marketable product or solution to a problem.	

Example

Consider this Qualitative Quantities IQuest on colonizing space. Humankind will continue to explore the possibilities for living beyond Earth, whether on a space station, on the moon, on Mars or beyond. Whether necessitated by conditions on Earth or the human drive to expand and conquer new frontiers, technology will eventually make the colonization of space a realistic goal. The Qualitative Quantities IQuest format does an excellent job of challenging student thinking on the requirements of successfully living beyond Earth, while employing a wide range of skills and concepts taught throughout the curriculum across grade levels.

Qualitative Quantities IQuest **Colonizing Space**	
EVENT	
Domain	Introspective
Intelligence(s)	Intrapersonal, Existential
Tasks	Discuss and share student values about life on Earth and the circumstances that would compel human-kind to create a community in space.
	Students generate a list of the things people need to lead healthy and happy lives.
	Challenge students to research the scientific and human requirements to live in space.
PROCESS	
Domain	Analytic
Intelligence(s)	Logical, Rhythmic, Naturalist
Tasks	Have students research information sources about living in space:
	• En route to Mars, the Moon: *www.nasa.gov/vision/universe/ solarsystem/18mar_moonfirst.html*
	• High School Space Settlement Design Competition: *http://spaceset.org*
	• International Space Station: *www.nasa.gov/ mission_pages/station/main/*
	• "Magic number" for space pioneers calculated: *www.newscientist.com/article/dn1936*
	• Red Colony: *www.redcolony.com*
	• Space Settlement: The Journey Inward: *www.space-settlement-institute.org/smwolfe/ ISDCtalk-stevewolfe.pdf*

Tasks (continued)	• Space Settlements: A Design Study: *www.nas.nasa.gov/About/Education/SpaceSettlement/75SummerStudy/Table_of_Contents1.html*
	• Why We Do—and Must—Go Into Space: *www.nsschapters.org/policy-cmte/files/WHY-JGL_302.pdf*
	Students identify, verify, and organize information.
	Students create a proposal for colonizing space.
PERFORMANCE	
Domain	Interactive
Intelligence(s)	Interpersonal, Linguistic
Tasks	Students format the proposal using original text and graphics.
	Students create a virtual tour of each proposed space colony, which can be delivered online.
	Post student presentations on a class space colonization website.

Characteristics

Notice the characteristics of this IQuest:

1. The introspective event sets the expectation for the IQuest.

2. The event and process contrast student beliefs with scientific fact.

3. The process immerses students in rationale and requirements for living in space.

4. The goal of the process is to create a viable space colony proposal that combines student values with practical considerations.

5. The proposal is not an end in itself; students must create a virtual tour of their proposed space colony.

6. Advanced students can create an interactive virtual tour.

7. Completed student work can be showcased on a class website.

The Qualitative Quantities IQuest helps students to not only apply research and information literacy skills, but to apply them within the context of human experience and values. The result is a vibrant celebration of human existence and the possibilities for the future.

The creation of virtual tours can be done using any of a variety of applications, from word processing and drawing programs to Glogster posters and digital video clips. At the high end, students may wish to create web pages or Flash animations that can illustrate their conceptions of life in their space colony.

Qualitative Quantities is an open-ended format that promotes imagination and creativity based on practical applications of understanding. There are many topics rich for exploration as Qualitative Quantities IQuests.

Correlation to the ISTE NETS for Students

This IQuest maps to all six standards:

1. Creativity and Innovation

Students demonstrate creative thinking, construct knowledge, and develop innovative products and processes using technology. Students:

b. create original works as a means of personal or group expression

2. Communication and Collaboration

Students use digital media and environments to communicate and work collaboratively, including at a distance, to support individual learning and contribute to the learning of others. Students:

> **b.** communicate information and ideas effectively to multiple audiences using a variety of media and formats

3. Research and Information Fluency

Students apply digital tools to gather, evaluate, and use information. Students:

> **a.** plan strategies to guide inquiry

> **c.** evaluate and select information sources and digital tools based on the appropriateness to specific tasks

4. Critical Thinking, Problem Solving, and Decision Making

Students use critical thinking skills to plan and conduct research, manage projects, solve problems, and make informed decisions using appropriate digital tools and resources. Students:

> **a.** identify and define authentic problems and significant questions for investigation

5. Digital Citizenship

Students understand human, cultural, and societal issues related to technology and practice legal and ethical behavior. Students:

> **b.** exhibit a positive attitude toward using technology that supports collaboration, learning, and productivity

6. Technology Operations and Concepts

Students demonstrate a sound understanding of technology concepts, systems, and operations. Students:

b. select and use applications effectively and productively

reflection

1. What is the role of human experience in the Information Age workplace?

2. How does the context of a problem change potential outcomes?

3. How does a Qualitative Quantities IQuest lend itself to using one's imagination?

4. Does a virtual tour have to be web based? Why?

CHAPTER 11

the
principle partners
IQuest
Information Literacy Meets Cultural Literacy

For all its ability to bring us closer together as a global
community, all technology is local. We experience everything we do online as it pertains to our daily lives. Think
about it: If a technology doesn't meet our personal needs
or fit into our community values, we don't make use of it.
Information literacy must include cultural literacy. Therefore,
it is always key to tie instructional technology to the pertinent needs and culture of the targeted audience with whom
we work. The closer technology matches our own unique
human experience, the more we will learn to use it successfully. This is as much an affective reality as a cognitive fact.
Too often, education foregoes the affective component of

learning. Multiple intelligences theory and technology bring this emotional aspect of intelligence back to the forefront in the discussion of how we teach and learn.

Structure

Introspective Event. The introspective domain emphasizes the affective component of learning. How do I perceive the world around me? What is important to me? What makes sense to me? How does my own experience compare to human experience in general? And how do I connect to the community around me? By placing the introspective intelligences in the IQuest event, participants are afforded the luxury of considering these questions at the outset of the problem-solving task at hand.

Interactive Process. The interactive domain in the IQuest process shifts personal awareness into action, launching students into activity by communicating and interacting with one another and with the world around them. With values and priorities in place, students are ready to learn more about the issue at hand through active learning. This can be done in a variety of environments from a self-contained classroom to an online community of practice.

Analytic Performance. The analytic domain in the IQuest performance brings closure to the IQuest by asking students to reflect on and respond to the learning experience in which they have engaged. The result is a collection of student work products that reflect on personal and communal values and celebrate human experience.

The structure, in template format, for a Principle Partners IQuest is shown on the next page.

Principle Partners IQuest		
Information Literacy Meets Cultural Literacy		
EVENT		
Domain	Introspective	
Intelligence(s)	Intrapersonal, Existential, Spatial	
Task	Reflect on personal and communal values.	
PROCESS		
Domain	Interactive	
Intelligence(s)	Interpersonal, Kinesthetic, Linguistic	
Task	Work with others to address a community issue.	
PERFORMANCE		
Domain	Analytic	
Intelligence(s)	Logical, Rhythmic, Naturalist	
Task	Assess collaborative work and present findings in a meaningful way.	

Example

Consider this Principle Partners IQuest on community oral history. Each generation leaves its own mark on the character of a city or town. In the past, much of the day-to-day history of a generation was lost if it was not written down as it happened. With today's technologies, local history no longer must be text-based or lost. We can capture the memories and stories of our parents and grandparents through interviews and digital audio and video recordings. This allows for meaningful dialogue between the generations that can be archived and shared for years to come.

Principle Partners IQuest **Community Oral History**	
EVENT	
Domain	Introspective
Intelligence(s)	Intrapersonal, Existential, Spatial
Tasks	Have students brainstorm the values and characteristics of the community they most prize.
	Create a class semantic map of the character and culture of the local community.
	Generate a list of community members who can share their memories of the community.
	Determine if there is more value in writing down, audio recording, or videorecording interviews with the community members listed.
PROCESS	
Domain	Interactive
Intelligence(s)	Interpersonal, Kinesthetic, Linguistic
Tasks	Have students work in teams of two or three to generate questions they would ask in interviewing community members about the history of their town.
	Have teams schedule interviews with members of the community willing to share their memories about the community throughout their life's time.
	Give each team a digital camcorder, MP3 recorder, or other digital recording device to use during their interviews.
	Upload completed interviews to a central virtual repository as they are completed; be sure that repository is backed up on a daily basis.

PERFORMANCE	
Domain	Analytic
Intelligence(s)	Logical, Rhythmic, Naturalist
Tasks	Have teams review one another's completed interviews.
	Students edit interviews as necessary.
	Students organize the collection of interviews by agreed upon categories and themes.
	Students post the completed collection of interviews on a class website as a community oral history archive.

Characteristics

Notice the characteristics of this IQuest:

1. The introspective event sets the expectation for the IQuest.

2. Student perception of their contemporary community impacts their sense of its past; social media tools can be used to help shape their perceptions.

3. Students have a choice in the media they use for the project, from audio podcasts to digital video, but they should all agree to use media formats consistently.

4. Students work in teams to share the tasks of conducting and recording successful interviews.

5. Systematic upload, storage, and back-up of interview files is critical.

6. Editing can be done in Audacity, Adobe Audition, Windows Movie Maker, Apple iMovie, or any other audio or video editor that meets your needs.

7. Interviews can be organized chronologically, topically, or by any other filter upon which students agree.

8. Web page development for archiving the interviews can be an extension of your existing class page or a separate, dedicated site to which your class site can link.

The Principle Partners IQuest is an excellent example of the seamless integration of technology into learning and productivity tasks. Higher-level technology integration is never about the technology; it operates incidentally to the task at hand.

Be sure to have each interviewee sign a media release statement indicating their permission for you to use their voice and/or image in your online oral history archive.

Making the finished interviews compatible for podcasting is an important goal to keep in mind in this project. Edited files should be saved in a format such as MP4 or QuickTime, so that they can be viewed and saved portably regardless of the platform or application of choice.

The Principle Partners IQuest makes a connection between what is possible and what is prized. In addition to personal values and interests, it is an excellent format for exploring social, ethical, and human issues related to technology, including its responsible use and positive attitudes that support it as a tool for lifelong learning.

Correlation to the ISTE NETS for Students

This IQuest maps to all six standards:

1. Creativity and Innovation

Students demonstrate creative thinking, construct knowledge, and develop innovative products and processes using technology. Students:

  b. create original works as a means of personal or group expression

2. Communication and Collaboration

Students use digital media and environments to communicate and work collaboratively, including at a distance, to support individual learning and contribute to the learning of others. Students:

  d. contribute to project teams to produce original works or solve problems

3. Research and Information Fluency

Students apply digital tools to gather, evaluate, and use information. Students:

  b. locate, organize, analyze, evaluate, synthesize, and ethically use information from a variety of sources and media

  c. evaluate and select information sources and digital tools based on the appropriateness to specific tasks

4. Critical Thinking, Problem Solving, and Decision Making

Students use critical thinking skills to plan and conduct research, manage projects, solve problems, and make

informed decisions using appropriate digital tools and resources. Students:

b. plan and manage activities to develop a solution or complete a project

5. Digital Citizenship

Students understand human, cultural, and societal issues related to technology and practice legal and ethical behavior. Students:

c. demonstrate personal responsibility for lifelong learning

6. Technology Operations and Concepts

Students demonstrate a sound understanding of technology concepts, systems, and operations. Students:

d. transfer current knowledge to learning of new technologies

reflection

1. Do you agree that all technology is local? Why or why not?

2. What are the values and traditions of your community?

3. Can information literacy be mastered without cultural literacy?

4. What technologies do you have at your disposal that would be conducive to a Principle Partners IQuest?

CHAPTER 12

multiple intelligences
and the
future of education

More than a decade into the new century, we are past talking about "21st-century" skills. We should be talking about what's after the 21st-century threshold. Consider the matrix I have created crossing two different axes that represent the major movements we are currently experiencing: the move from ingesting information to acquiring insight, and the move from seeing the larger global context to actually creating and inhabiting global communities (Figure 12.1).

The new century is characterized first and foremost by an information explosion. At the outset, the challenge seemed to be to simply be able to manage the data with which we are inundated. But as the tools to manage data have become more and more user-friendly, the next challenge is to find contexts for the pertinent information we encounter—context provided by the experience and expertise we bring to understanding information. When we have meaningful understanding of *information*, *insight* is created, the kind of insight that identifies opportunities for innovation. The x axis on the matrix reflects the shift from mere information management to insight.

The second major change we are experiencing is movement from the simple realization that we live in a global economy to actively contributing to a communal marketplace of ideas. The first decade of the 21st century kicked off with a celebration of the fact that we now have the capability to interact globally, and we have been doing that through various electronic communications. But with this capability now demonstrated daily, the next challenge is to use these tools to truly build communities across traditional geographic and political boundaries. It is slowly taking place as we bridge the challenges of time zones, language differences, and cultural differences. The y axis on the matrix represents a shift from simple *global awareness to collaborating communities* worldwide.

The resulting four quadrants complete the matrix:

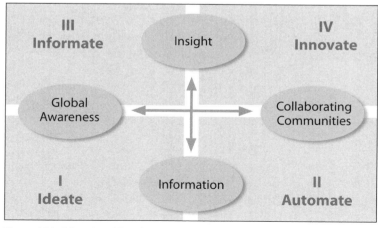

Figure 12.1 Educational Paradigm Matrix

Ideate Paradigm. Quadrant I is the Ideate paradigm: generating ideas based on global information. This is where the 21st century started. It is the result of norm-referenced standardized testing and the push to compare ourselves not only with local students, but students elsewhere. The institutional reaction to how students compare to others around the world generates entirely new initiatives to close gaps and document student achievement improvement. This approach is linear and sequential and focused on deficits. It is Zeno's "racetrack paradox," which states that if you keep advancing half the distance to the finish line, mathematically you never actually reach it (Aristotle, *Physics* 239b11-13). This is the rut in which education sits today, and because it is statistically impossible to ever reach the finish line, public education has become politicized and polarized. No one wins.

Automate Paradigm. Quadrant II is the Automate paradigm. Digital technology has allowed us to complete a number of traditional tasks faster, more accurately, and with greater ease than we used to be able to accomplish the same tasks in the industrial age. This has been a huge breakthrough in productivity and efficiency. Unfortunately it has also made technology a primary focus in-and-of itself. Automating our schools does not transform education; it simply builds on the ways we already teach with new tools used to complete traditional goals. Of particular concern is the role vendors are now playing in education decision-making; the lines have blurred and we are not necessarily making educational decisions based solely on the needs of the learner. There is now an insidious commercial influence that has the potential to move public education into the domain of private enterprise.

Informate Paradigm. Quadrant III is the Informate paradigm. Using digital communications and learning tools, we can create new ways to empower every family to support their children as learners. Instead of focusing on the technology, transform education by building capacity for all family members, students, *and* parents, to be active lifelong learners. This paradigm transcends automating, looking past immediate task-focused instructional goals and focusing on a global destination for public education: The more school-aged families become acclimated to using information portals, electronic communications and online learning communities, the more we will realize our mission in public education to provide a free, appropriate education for everyone. In this paradigm we elevate the impact of education by engaging all education stakeholders using the tools we have at our disposal.

Innovate Paradigm. Quadrant IV is the Innovate paradigm. Beyond generating ideas, automating tasks, and informating electronically, innovating is the ultimate goal: generating original knowledge, new products, and novel solutions to problems that are valued across learning communities. To innovate is to push the envelope, take risks, gain insight, and eventually break new ground that contributes to the greater good. Risks that do not produce innovation are not considered failures, but opportunities to gain insight for future risk-taking, as well. Find a point on the horizon where you know you and your students must be and then use the insight you possess to figure out how to get there. As a result of reaching that point on the horizon, the worldwide economy is infused with energy and ideas and new possibilities. This is the future today's children will inherit, and we must prepare them for it.

So, rather than fixating on 21st-century skills, identify where you are now on the matrix and then figure out your next steps to help your students and school and community move forward toward innovating. Do you have to go through each paradigm as they are sequenced on the matrix? No. The matrix is simply a high-level snapshot of where we are and where we are headed. Instead of trying to match the matrix step-for-step, practice true innovating by finding the point on the horizon where you know you need to be—a model innovator—and then work to gain insight on how you will get there. Take risks based on your insight, and learn from your journey.

How do we summarize the journey to innovating? From an education perspective, we need to revolutionize the ways we work, the ways we teach, and the ways we learn. We cannot simply reform the old model. We must transform public education into a new, global, innovating enterprise that becomes the engine for a revitalized economy.

Technology is intregal in both converting raw data (information) into understanding (insight) and bridging the gap between comparing ourselves to other cultures (global awareness) to participating in new societies (collaborating communities). Although the focus can't be on the technology itself, we as educators must be looking for the ways the technology can open possibilities for our students to learn.

Of course, the focus always comes back to students learning. Melding our understanding of how the world is changing, how technology is providing opportunity, and a sound understanding of the multiple intelligences is a roadmap that can lead our educational system not only deep into the 21st century, but well beyond.

national educational technology standards for students (nets•s)

All K–12 students should be prepared to meet the following standards and performance indicators.

1. Creativity and Innovation

Students demonstrate creative thinking, construct knowledge, and develop innovative products and processes using technology. Students:

a. apply existing knowledge to generate new ideas, products, or processes

b. create original works as a means of personal or group expression

c. use models and simulations to explore complex systems and issues

d. identify trends and forecast possibilities

2. Communication and Collaboration

Students use digital media and environments to communicate and work collaboratively, including at a distance, to support individual learning and contribute to the learning of others. Students:

a. interact, collaborate, and publish with peers, experts, or others employing a variety of digital environments and media

b. communicate information and ideas effectively to multiple audiences using a variety of media and formats

c. develop cultural understanding and global awareness by engaging with learners of other cultures

d. contribute to project teams to produce original works or solve problems

3. Research and Information Fluency

Students apply digital tools to gather, evaluate, and use information. Students:

a. plan strategies to guide inquiry

b. locate, organize, analyze, evaluate, synthesize, and ethically use information from a variety of sources and media

c. evaluate and select information sources and digital tools based on the appropriateness to specific tasks

d. process data and report results

4. Critical Thinking, Problem Solving, and Decision Making

Students use critical-thinking skills to plan and conduct research, manage projects, solve problems, and make informed decisions using appropriate digital tools and resources. Students:

a. identify and define authentic problems and significant questions for investigation

b. plan and manage activities to develop a solution or complete a project

c. collect and analyze data to identify solutions and make informed decisions

d. use multiple processes and diverse perspectives to explore alternative solutions

5. Digital Citizenship

Students understand human, cultural, and societal issues related to technology and practice legal and ethical behavior. Students:

a. advocate and practice the safe, legal, and responsible use of information and technology

b. exhibit a positive attitude toward using technology that supports collaboration, learning, and productivity

c. demonstrate personal responsibility for lifelong learning

d. exhibit leadership for digital citizenship

6. Technology Operations and Concepts

Students demonstrate a sound understanding of technology concepts, systems, and operations. Students:

a. understand and use technology systems

b. select and use applications effectively and productively

c. troubleshoot systems and applications

d. transfer current knowledge to the learning of new technologies

© 2007 International Society for Technology in Education (ISTE), www.iste.org. All rights reserved.

DATE DUE

PRINTED IN U.S.A.